Today, Grayson and vacuum learned all about our planet. Mrs. Bee says it is our responsibility to take good care of earth.

She tells us that earth is feeling sick because there are too many trapped gases in the atmosphere surrounding earth. When this happens, the earth begins to warm up.

"We share our planet with many plants and animals," Grayson says.

"That is correct Grayson," says Mrs. Bee.

OZONE LAYER

The  is our habitat, and it is also home to many plants and animal species. We must take good care of our earth so that it will last a long time.

"I know an example," says vacuum. "After we play mommy tells us to pick up our toys, or the floor will be a big mess and we will have nowhere to walk."

"That's correct," says Mrs. Bee. "If we do not clean up the earth now, future generations may have no place to live."

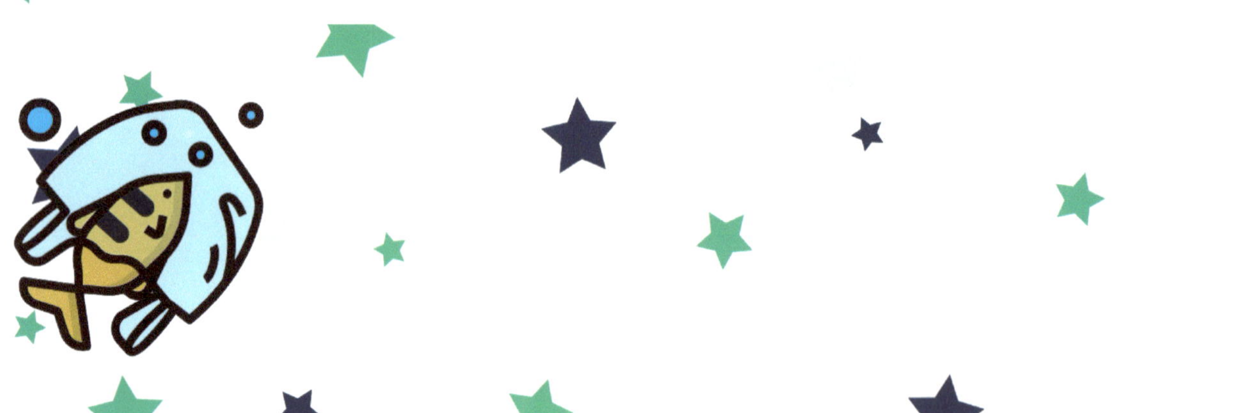

Some human activity might be to blame for earth's changes because many people are not recycling, instead, they are throwing trash on the ground, driving cars that add smoke to the air and chopping down our forests.

Some days are incredibly sad because the sun is too hot, and the factories are releasing too much black smoke into the air.

"Smoke makes the sky turn dark!" says Grayson.

"You are correct," says Mrs. Bee.

Grayson remembers an extremely hot day when his ice cubes melted before he could make a glass of lemonade.

Kathy remembers when her ice cream cone melted before she could eat it.

Chris remembers his ice frosty melting too fast.

At the beach Tammy found a sad little turtle with a plastic bag stuck on its neck.

These are all examples of what happens with climate change.

Factories, cars and trucks cause lots of pollution to enter the air. Big black puffs of smoke rise and turn the blue skies gray.

"On a gray day, you cannot see the mountains," said Tammy.

Another thing that causes pollution is when we use plastic and forget to recycle. It may end up in our oceans and harm the animals. Like the turtle Tammy found. Some animals even swallow plastic and this is harmful.

SCHOOL BUS

When the earth is too warm, the ocean water heats up and the ice caps begin to melt. This is not good for some animals that live in this habitat. One baby polar bear is separated from its mommy. He begins to cry.

"Oh no," says Grayson. "The ice is melting, and the polar bears will have no place to live soon."

If the earth keeps heating up, the oceans will get warmer making the ice melt. This causes the sea levels to rise, and many animals will lose their homes.

"Let's take a trip into space to get a better look at the problem!" says vacuum.

Soon they are on their way to another adventure. Grayson and vacuum mount their rocket ship and **BLAST OFF** into space!

They want to get a closer look at the ozone layer, they must help the planet the best way they can.

COMET
VENUS
MOON
MERCURY
EARTH
SUN

They pass by many planets. Can you name them?

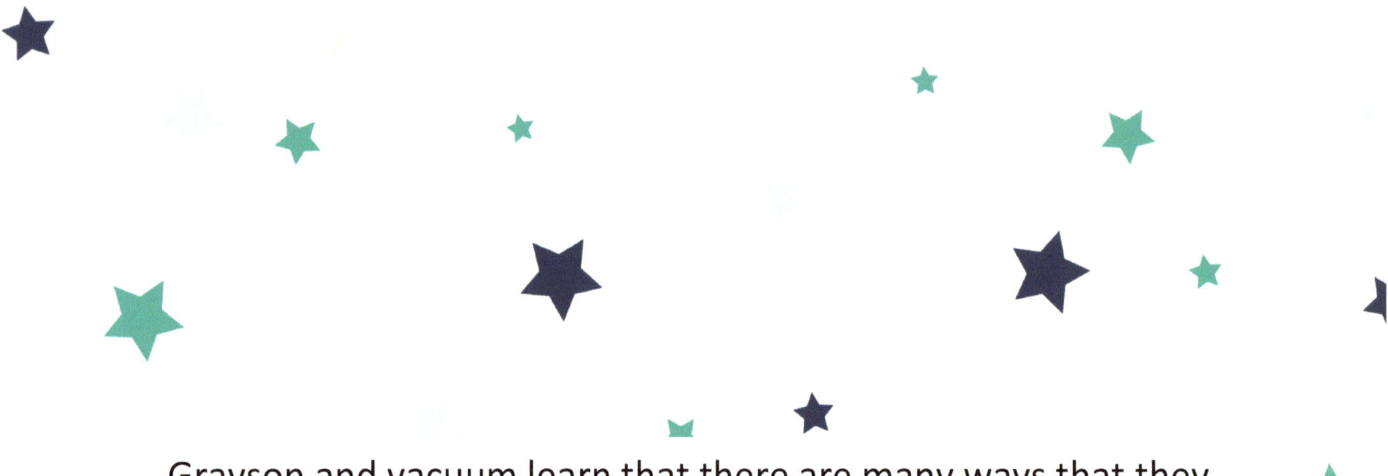

Grayson and vacuum learn that there are many ways that they

can help to protect earth. There are ways you to help too!

TURN OFF
LIGHTS
RECYCLE
TRASH

USE LESS
WATER
RIDE YOUR
BICYCLE
OR
WALK

"We can all begin by picking up trash and recycling!" says

Grayson. You can begin at home and in your own neighborhood.

"We can also do our part by planting trees!" says Kathy.

"Trees produce oxygen, and we need to breath fresh air!"

After cleaning up the beach, Grayson and Tammy send turtle

back to the ocean to swim freely.

"What about the baby polar bear?" asks vacuum.

"We can help him too," says Grayson. "Pull!"

Vacuum turns his motor on full speed and together he and Grayson pull baby polar bear closer.

"Horraaayyy!" mama polar bear cheers.

"Yipeeee!" baby polar bear giggles with glee.

Together they reunite mama and baby polar bear.

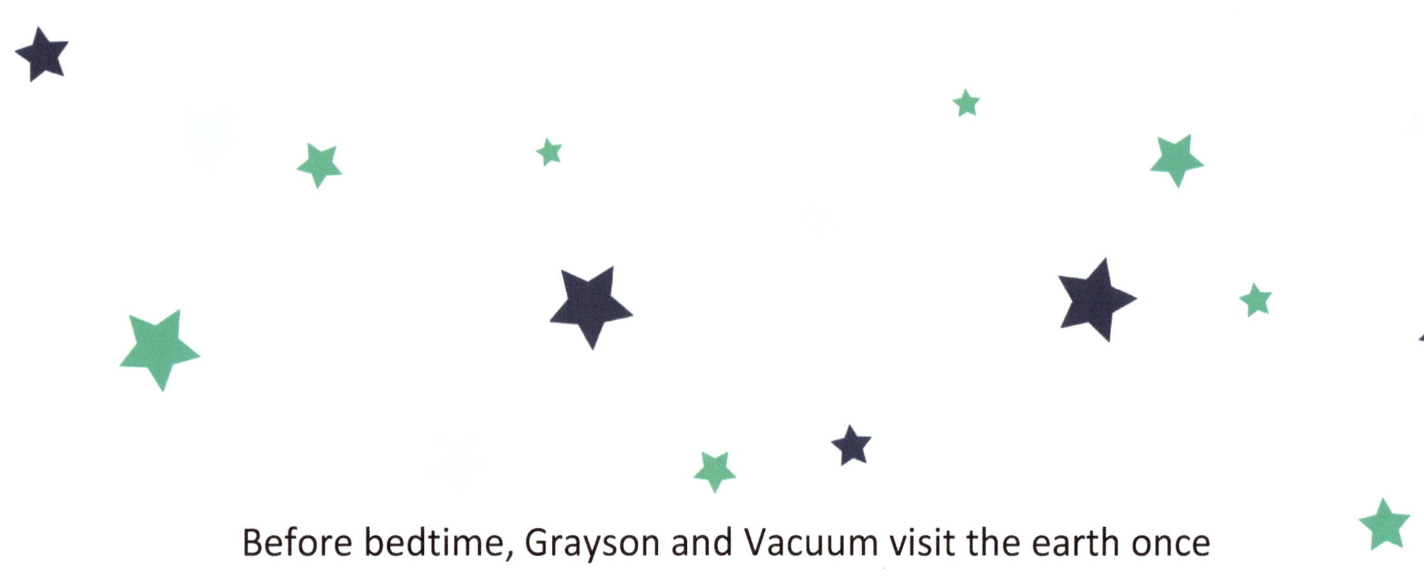

Before bedtime, Grayson and Vacuum visit the earth once more and with their help and yours the earth can smile again!

Did you know that April 22 of each year is Earth Day? Many people volunteer to help clean on earth day.

Happy
Earth
Day

Learn the colors that help:
Orange
Green
Blue
Gray
Yellow
Red

PLASTIC
GLASS
PAPER
ORGANIC
METAL
E-WASTE

Your positive Review on Amazon will keep me writing. Please help me to bring more books to your child.

Also, check out other books in the Goodnight Vacuum Series

Can you think of more ways we can help to protect earth?

www.kimberlyezabiaartis.com

Rocketship

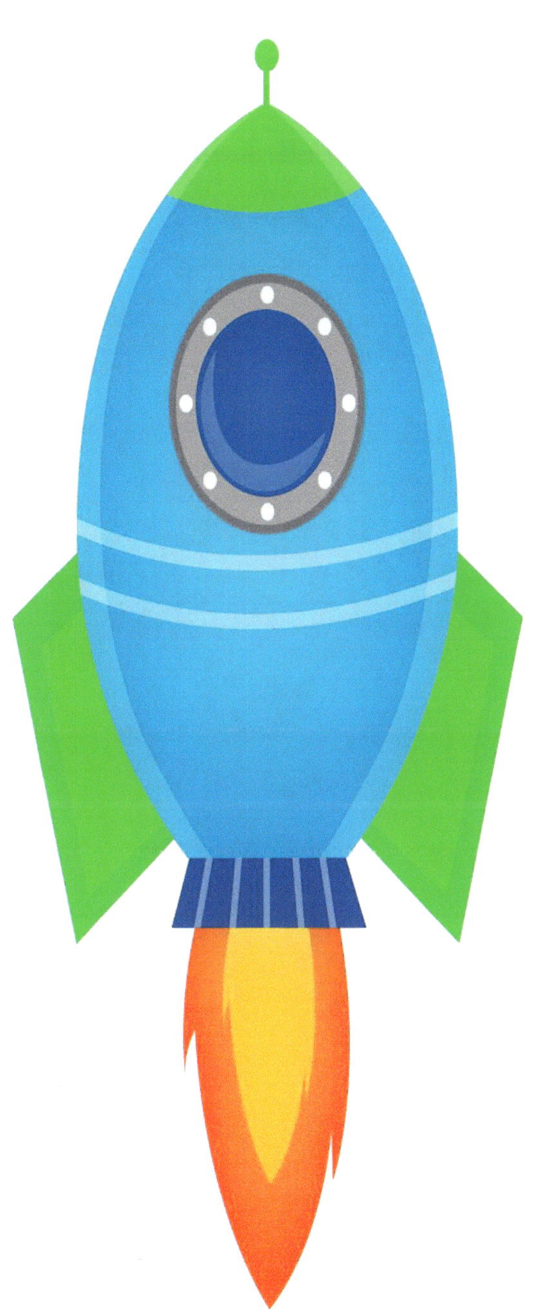

Astronaut

find the correct shadow

how
many

how
many

find 5 differences

find the correct shadow

find 2 same pictures